WHERE YOU ARE! 2
LIT UP YOUR LAMP.

NINGTHOUJAM BASANTA SINGH (THOUREN)

BlueRose ONE.com
Stories Matter
NewDelhi • London

BLUEROSE PUBLISHERS
India | U.K.

For permissions requests or inquiries regarding this publication, please contact:

BLUEROSE PUBLISHERS
www.BlueRoseONE.com
info@bluerosepublishers.com
+91 8882 898 898
+4407342408967

ISBN: 978-93-7310-601-4

Cover design: Aman Sharma
Typesetting: Manisha Rawat

First Edition: December 2025

Where You Are! - II

LIT UP YOUR LAMP

PREFACE

Everyone wants to strive for success and happiness in life. An undisciplined mind makes a man slave and wrecks of life. Controlling and subduing turbulent mind is vexing problem to the earnest seeker of success and happiness. Your dream is most important in achieving your happiness and success.

I, just, share some of my knowledge. This will make all readers, and who get the information will grow and become rich.

Therefore, I share my ideas under the inspirations of "The Blue Rose Publishers". This publisher gave me a lot of motivation to draft my book. Thanks to the Blue Rose publishes for giving me all round inspiration.

I thought I was not a writer. How I can author a book. This is not possible for me to write such a book.

However, with the help of encouragement from Blue Rose Publishers I write this book with the thought that I can contribute something to the people what I can as a human being. Why I am born, what my duty is! On thinking this, 1 started writing of this book to the completion.

Everybody has a profession of his own liking, say, some may like painting, writings, dancing, sports, crafts, doctors, civil service many more. However, one may like two or more professions at a same time, yes, he can do all the professions.

But many people live without a proper job. People living in the hazard life without jobs, not knowing what to do and how to start.

Therefore, I suggest some way how to do it, how he will get. It is for both men and women. As I really met in my life the disadvantages, and advantage, weal or woes in the life's journey. Everybody will definitely face this problem in life. Therefore, I suggest that those who are left from Govt. jobs and having no passive income, can do and start earning income for building passive income house.

In the following chapters I relate what I have experienced; it is real-life's happening. Whether you like it or not, you'll have to face it – the following chapters explain what reality really is in life and how to build up a success, happy life.

In writing this book, my daughter, Ningthoujam Wangthoibi, helped me in correcting errors and in reshaping the work into its present form.

I read hundreds of books on motivations and career; I refer to Jim Cathcart. Acorn principles, Napoleon Hills' book on success are good as well. These books will motivate you in your career and in building up your business. They help me to improve my life.

I refer to these books in the view of fact that it will motivate you in your way to success. Your profession and creativity are particularly important in life's success.

I mainly give emphasis on business for success in life. Being business as career offers greater freedom and flexibility... Success in business makes able to manage your life.

Eighty percent of the world population live in tread mill's way of life -despite working hard but continued living in same condition and no visible improvement in life. We work the hardest, but we live poor.

However, 20% of the world's population live in a good life. Their lifestyle and comfort are different from the people who work hardest but living in poor condition.

I hope we can change our lifestyle to 20% people lifestyle. Then our human society can change to a better society.

Contents

CHAPTER – 1
PROFESSIONS

We have natural values.

According to Jim Cathcart - he gives seven natural values. According to these natural values we will make to choose our profession. Profession in another word is career or occupation which you will do it as your life's career. It is also related to your earning of money. Some may do a profession not related to earning money. But I give emphasis on earning money for livelihood or a better life. Different people do different professions.

We may find out our profession with our natural values and natural intelligence.

Natural values are:

Sensuality- the relative inclination to one's physical experience – comfort, adjustment of things, a person will be discussing about palate gourmet of dining to enjoy taste, food texture, the smells, etc. They are consistent with doing food business, fashion clothes or anything that are related to their sensuality.

Empathy: Your inclination, importance of feeling connected to people - say social works. Service to humanity - like Mother Teresa, Doctors, etc.

Next is wealth- Your values to wealth and worth - You love money, wealth - so it is big businessperson. They love to earn money, to posses' wealth of great values.

Another value is Aesthetics- it is relative importance on beauty, balance, order, and symmetry -for this such professions as Artists, Engineers, Architecture, etc.

Next is knowledge - It is your inclination towards loving of writing, reading, thinking you love accumulation of knowledge.

Last value is Commitment - This value is relative useful in all above values. But it is not business profession. However, it is particularly important in performing our work, your career better.

Moreover, you have some natural intelligence:

1. Verbal intelligence (word/smart) - It is related to words, language skills. If you have this ability that - to think and communicate in verbal terms - you become politicians, public speaker, etc.

2. Visual intelligence - Picture smart - you have the capacity to visualise, an ability to think in terms of shapes and arrangement of things, to see symbols, etc. It is related to artists, designers, cinematography, etc.

3. Physical intelligence - Body smart - It relates to physical movement, ability to think in terms of movements, ability to think with your body, to understand things via physical involvement with things; hand on knowing : sports, arts, sculptures, play about with, adjustment, tinkering, gardening, dance, body building, travelling, etc.

4. Musical intelligence - You have the ability to know music, rhythm, resonance, vibrations to sounds of nature - simply, singing, playing guitar, violins, drumming, etc.

5. Next is mathematical intelligence or logic. It is concerned with your ability to do with numbers, geometric designs, problem solving and analysis. Such as puzzles, mysteries, calculating, logic: Mathematicians, physicist, lawyers, etc.

6. Interpersonal Intelligence - you are an excellent communicator. You love to socialise with all kinds of different people. Example foreign services, diplomat, volunteer works, moderator, etc. It is good for business performance.

7. Intrapersonal Intelligence - It is ability to look inside yourself and thing yourself. They're the least team oriented. They like isolation. They mostly like to read and write books: Thinkers and philosophers have that tendencies.

Now, I say the above discussion for choosing one's profession is not that hard and fast standards. It is simply a suggestion for your choices of profession.

It is your profession that will sustain your livelihood. That will make your life financially sound. So, everybody needs a profession of his choices. It is for his service and well earnings.

So, all people have different inclinations on different traits on different degrees. So, according to their likings as they have different values and different intelligences, choice is theirs. Some may like, doctors, engineers, computers, other may prefer to social works, sports, Art and also some may like business. For me I prefer to business.

Now choose your profession according to your natural inclinations. However, I will discuss mainly on business.

CHAPTER – 2
CREATIVITY

People love assorted designs, different tastes of foods, clothes, cars, decorations, etc. So, creativity makes satisfaction to people's hungry and love of unique styles of products, variety of tastes as it does to the sensual persons.

So, people who are creative and create many new things, for customer choices we see today innumerable things on art, on products. It is a continuous work. It makes the world change.

How will you create new things, food of different flavour and styles; so, expose too many things relating to your chosen profession you will get perspectives of your exposures. Then you will form new ideas. Your brain and neurones work incessantly day and night. Your creativity or idea of creating things with flash suddenly. It may happen while you write, read, work, look, eat, walk and during meditation also. Remember, be ready to note down your ideas anytime because it escapes very quickly.

You need many trials for production of new things. More and more activities and a-lot of exposures you need to approach for forming new ideas (creating new things) for example in the field of engineering – architecture, the engineers have to see, enquire many designs shapes, colours, structures, angles etc. for finding a new design: house, bridges, etc.

Considering paintings - you might see many paintings of great artists, their brush strokes, colour combination, giving shades and placing of things, the impressions they want to give. You go to see many exhibitions, and art galleries. Recollect them in your mind. Do it repeatedly your subconscious mind will work for you.

As you do this a sudden flash of new ideas will come to you in your mind. Then note it carefully, repetition of flash of ideas coming to you is extraordinary.

As I am very much concerned mainly for the average people who consisted of 80% of the world population (that I will explain it Average people - in the later chapter) I like to suggest you create more ideas in your production areas. Such as food, clothes, cane products, weed products, etc.

You know Newton, Thomas Edison, Henry Ford, they did this trial and error hundred and thousands of times. They failed they tried till their trial worked.

In food, different and varieties foods are beings increasingly produced day by day likewise cane and weed products also do. We love to eat many foods with different tastes/flavours, colours, texture, cooking styles, aroma etc.

So, you expose in them as possible as you can. Here exposure I mean see, taste, smell, many different products; habit is also one important factor in this aspect. When you do a thing repeatedly, you will form habit of doing it. Remember - form a good habit, then it will become a part of nature of yours.

Another thing your brain to make creative is to put things together and making rearrangement of these things and changing Again. By doing so you will form a new idea, example:

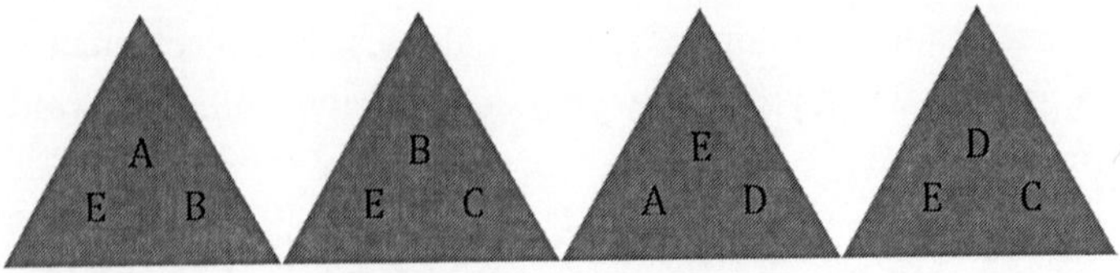

When you rearrange things like above new idea will be formed. Take in information into your brain, your Brain will work for you incessantly. New ideas will flash in an instant, it may happen while you walk or work, listening to music, reading books, in sleeping and so and so. Don't forget to write it down when it comes.

CHAPTER – 3
SPIRITUALITY

Mind never allows a vacuum. You will think continuously anything as you put ideas, forms, events, etc. in your mind. These will form you, your mind.

Love everyone. Don't hate. Love arises in the mind, and it vanishes from the mind again. Hate also does the same thing. If hate manifest the longer, if harms the mind and body. So, control hatred, anger. Sitting silently specially in the morning on any time when you are free from work. Try to think one subject as you think feel pleasant. You are absorbed in that pleasant thought. You may sometimes feel floating in that thought forgetting your body consciousness. You may be fear of losing of your body consciousness. Do not fear. It will not last long. When you come down to your normal consciousness you will feel relaxed and happy.

Love, anger, hatred, envious, jealousy (emotions) are all inside you. The only thing you will do is to control them. When love arises, most of the time, it attracts more good things to you. It will attract people, money, sympathy, many more things. It develops happiness and good health. Practice to develop love, affection.

Try hard to avoid anger, hatred, jealousy (negative feelings) when they arise, through reason, discipline, and practice, Meditation will help to control these emotions.

Today the world, most people are attracted to material comfort and pleasures. They have no time in taking spiritual engagement.So I am simply repeating this.

Spiritual masters, saint, sages already taught this. If we are moving towards to get happiness. If we do not do spiritual disciplines, sadhanas. So, we suffer. Self-control, discipline are the best way to achieve happiness. The best way to achieve happiness. Yes, almost all living things are territorial by nature, therefore, they fight each other to control some area, some possession. The same thing we human being also do. We want to possess land, buildings, money because of fear of being poor, and loss of security,

There are many factors for attaining happiness. Yes, spirituality alone cannot make us happy. We need food, clothing, interacting among ourselves the weal or woes of our lives.

However, spirituality clears our mind, it also clears our ways to go. It also gives us what to do and not to do in our social interactions, and in the achievement of our dreams.

Spirituality guides us what to do and what not to do. It is a very important factor in the achievement of happiness. It empowers our concentration in performing our goals.

Without spirituality our goal (dream) cannot be perfect. Spirituality in my concept is honesty, discipline, loving life, however I shall not go deeper into the concept of getting emancipation, salvation of God in the idea of or through spiritualism. It is not my way to investigate spiritualism in the sense of God seeking because I am not a religions seeker of God realisation.

If anybody like to go ahead in spiritualism (God connection) do religious practices, such as yoga, kundalini, and reading of religious books and satsanga, etc. Here, my idea on spiritualism is to touching spiritual disciplines. It is a must in the journey of attaining happiness, success in mundane life.

Spirituality is very much related with our professions, creativity and earning of money. Concentration is a part of well performance in our works. Deeper thinking in our works we can make creativity.

Spirituality gives us more understanding of our lives and also our lives with others, our relations with other. We are all related each other in some way or other. Using this relationship tediously, we get more advantage in our development as well as other lives.

CHAPTER – 4
MONEY OR FINANCE

Why we will do all these practices of spirituality and relationships. It is because of happiness. Happiness depends much on spirituality and relationships. Yes, spirituality and relationships alone cannot make us happy. The another factor for attaining happiness is Money or financial skill.

Let us have a brief study about finance and how to get money and why we want money. Just after the chapter on Health, other chapters are centred round how to get money and financial prosperity, and factors involve in attaining financial house.

Money satisfies our wants and gives pleasure as we enter into the material world. It gives us safety and security. So, everybody wants money. Some are mad in earning more and more money. Money is a very powerful tool to get what we want in this life. However, I don't discuss here much about the free money. I discuss and say about the hard-earned money. Money can be classified into hard earned money and easy money.

Easy money comes and goes away quickly. No one knows how to retain it. One in thousand and ten thousand may retain easy money because they suffered much in life for the lack of money.

It is exceptional to retain free money for longer period of time.

Here is a story: "There is no free launch in life".

There was a wise king in a country who thought of the future of prosperity and living happily of his subjects. He called his pandits, courtiers to his assembly and said them to write a book for the future generation. The book should contain the knowledge and experience of all ages. He said that those who could write that book would get huge amount of gold coins as reward.

The learned courtiers and pandits agreed the king for the work. They went back home. They discussed and studied a lot of books. After one month they submitted to the king a voluminous book that contained knowledge of all ages. The wise king rejected it and told them that it was too lengthy. And he said, "Try to compress it". Then the learn courtiers and pandits went back and they discussed more among themselves to shorten the book. They could do it. They brought the book to the King, in the form of 100 pages book. Still the King wasn't satisfied with that.

The King said to the learned courtiers and pandits that it (book) was good but asked to try to shorten the book more, because people would skim over most of the pages without reading them. Then the exhausted pandits and courtiers thought how to do it. Desired to own the pleasure of the reward and fame. They even tried it again and after some months they brought the book to the king in the form of a page. However, the wise King asked the courtiers and pandits to shorten it more.

Then, the disappointed courtiers and pandits tried it again. They did not give up their effort. After some months they brought the book of all knowledge and of all ages in the form of one paragraph and submitted it to the king. The wise King was then happy. Still, he insisted the courtiers and pandits to shorten it more. The worried pandits and courtiers went back home as they did not give up their hope. After some month they brought it and presented it to the king. It was in the form of one sentence.

The one sentence book was in hand of the King. The wise King saw it and was very happy to see one sentence book. It was written," There is no free launch in life". The King exclaimed," longer the book, the people will not read it; shorter the book people would retain it by heart".

They all were satisfied and, the courtiers and pandits were rewarded.

Now the story illustrates that the hard earned wealth only offer true satisfaction, so people must work hard.

Hard earned money is best.

Life's journey is curve, people always think when money start to come; money will always come to them. No, it is a false concept. Flow of money sometimes rise and sometimes falls. So, save money for your down times.

REMEMBER, save your money for down times. Manage your money for your safety.

Work hard, be patient, be resilient, earn money. As you know money satisfies our wants. It gives you security. We like continuous money flow to us. Continuous small flow of income is called passive income. But I will discuss how to earn passive income and possibilities of getting capital for earning passive income, in the coming chapters.

Reserve your money, food and essential commodities. We cannot predict the detour of life that may happen out time. Again I state to save money, save dry food for future.

Okay, we need money to buy house, motor cars, good clothes, lastly food and make pleasures and many more. So, we get good living and happy life by having more money and by using it. This is time. But you know money only cannot bring us a happy life. We require good health to enjoy our lives.

Remember one thing: Nowadays business becomes a way of life. Failing in business will mean failure of our lives. One time it was for common people but nowadays, business means management of our lives.

Many popular and great men failed in…... lives, the management of money. So, they go through I trouble water in the run of life journey.

So, it is very important in our lives to skilfully manage our money without shortage of it.

CHAPTER – 5
HEALTH

Our body is a precious gift of nature. We need to take care of it carefully. So, heath is a particularly important part is our discussion. We need good health to enjoy our lives. So, health is important factor for attainment of happy life. In the journey of life good health takes a fundamental role. Without good health we cannot enjoy money we have earned hard.

Modern times' complexity of health issues increases. We need to go to doctors, health experts often to check up and improve our health. Meditation, spirituality is very much related with issue of good health. If you are ill, you cannot work. If you cannot work you stop earning money. Although you have a considerable sum of money you cannot enjoy your money when you are ill and have bad health. Therefore, keep your health to the maximum level of healthiness. Clean every part of your body fingers, nails, legs, eyes, face, head, teeth, skins. Body and souls love to take care of them. Do it.

So, take foods for good health: Such as fish, egg, mustard oil, leave, pumpkin, green peas, carrot, eggplant, cabbage, cauliflower, gourd, lotus seeds, yongchak (stink beans) , peas, mint, so and so.

I suggest more: banana, apples, goose berry, olive, heibi and fruits which are less acidic. Milk, palak, coconut and its water, avocado fruit, guava, pomegranate etc.

Regarding meat - do not take it much - it is not suitable for our human digestive system.

Remember, there are certain foods which are not suitable to your body. See it and avoid them. For example, I am Ningthoujam Clan (blood) - (our blood) we are forbidden to eat eel fish. After some year, my teeth was broken and teeth weak because I ate eel without heeding much attention to our elders' advice.

So, it needs further research, examinations for why.

Certain people are suitable for certain foods and good for them. Therefore, take food according to your suitability and healthy maintenance of your body.

Further, we have to pay our attention to vitamins and minerals. Lack of vitamins and minerals causes our body weak and illness. Nowadays, in most cases when we are ill, doctors prescribe to take vitamins and minerals.

I also suggest taking vitamins and minerals for your good health. Take vitamins, minerals frequently. But consult doctors and health experts before you take it.

However, there is controversy among doctors and experts on this subject about taking food supplements (vitamins, minerals, protein, etc.) still people take as I do to take regularly. I am not health expert so I shall not go further on this matter.

Do exercise at least 30 minutes every day to let your sweat out of your body, to let out poisonous parts from your body. Exercise, walking can do it.

Do spiritual sadhana in the morning or any time you get free time. Morning is best time. And take foods as I suggested above. Take food according to your suitability to your body system. Always maintain good health to enjoy your life and to use your hard-earned money in enjoyable, pleasurable, happily way of life. Note: Simple Food is best for Good Heath.

CHAPTER – 6
RELATIONSHIPS

As social being we need to live together depending on each other. Our family set up, our neighbours living harmoniously to make our lives progressively happily, joyously depend very much on this relationship. Balancing this relationship makes us get what we want happiness and peace.

If, we quarrel, have grudge with neighbours and friends and if we have sad relations with friends and neighbours, this is not a good sign of our lives to live happily and peacefully.

Yes, different minds, different thinking we have, we are all different. But we also have some or more similarities in our characters. Viewpoints, we need to nurture, develop these similarities and make more viewpoints be included in our similarities. We call it adjustment. Differences in our likings, views make us frequent disputes and quarrels, argument on our interests. Egos take part a great role in this fight, tussles. So, save your time by abandoning, avoiding quarrels, tussles, fight, anger, hatred as possible as you can.

I know these quarrels, hatred, anger, etc. (bad emotions) will surely happen to you in your life. But our purpose is to achieve our goals. So we should try to control our bad emotions.

For this we require training of mind. As I said earlier that the spirituality will make us able to control these bad feelings.

Always try to calm down your emotions. Bad emotions accrue to nothing good. Try to bring up your inner strength, the strength to control it, reason why do that quarrel and fight benefit you.

Reason what is the gain from it. If no reason is found, you avoid from it. Cut off relationship from them till you get a new understanding in future with them. Dialogue, negotiation can be helpful to being understanding.

Remember your time factor is very important to bring your success.

Now let us make a list of past friends, friends while you were a little boy and girls. You had many friends whom you played joyously, dined together, etc. Make a list of them and try to connect with them. It is possible as we now live in advanced technology age such as to communicate through telegram, email, social media platforms, etc. Through telephone or other means try to call and connect and chat with them.

Next, your present friends and future friends

Make the list of present friends, so also future friends particularly rich people who would be your customer and investor. Then tick them in order of importance.

In building up relationships we have diverse types of people, I hope it will be helping to understand these types of people in building relationships.

I just learned this from Jim Cathcart books (The Acorn principles)

Types of personalisation: But it is without proper demarcated lines. It means that they have overlapping characters.

Relaters are loyal, attentive pleasant, smooth (mellow), patient, cooperative and pleasant. It is negative side are indecisive, immobile possessive, hesitant and poor delegators.

Socialisers: They are open and trustworthy enthusiastic optimistic, etc.

One the negative side they are more emotional easily persuaded gullible (trust without sufficient evidence), highly talkative, imprecise, etc.

Thinkers: They tend to be orderly, precise conscientious, neat, trustworthy and careful.

In negative side they are a bit fearful, dependent, defensive, traditional, restrained and inexpressive.

Director - They tend to be leaders; they are good at initiating, and competitive showing confident and forceful personality powerful, assertive. Its negative side is impulsive, forceful, pushy, inattentive, impatient, etc.

Therefore, the above brief types of people and its natures we will count in building our relationships.

Now make, the list of people particularly rich people, and people who will be a great customer for you. Try to close to them. Remember that the more you give the more you. Try it.

Always see in your jobs, meeting people, what is inside for you. If you get opportunity, then think also what you will give to or share to others. It will improve your relationship.

Taking only from other what you want and not willing to give on share to other will not develop your relationship. Help people. Giving and sharing what you have, and you can be also a good policy to improve your relationship.

Another important thing is that if you are producer. Try to buy from dukan (shops) from particular selects of shopkeepers. There will be attachment between you and shopkeepers. Then when you asked them to sell your products, they will accept you. 90% sure. Now let us build up, our business.

CHAPTER – 7
START UP YOUR BUSINESS

Here, I refer business. It means mainly the production, buying and selling. You can produce varieties of products for example - cake, cane products such as chairs, bags, dish wash, pen, pencils, etc. etc. For production you need money. You need money to buy materials for production, Sure! How to get money! It is a headache for everyone. As I did in my struggle for my life's sustainability. Money, Money! We have to invest money for earning money.

Knock the door it will open, seek you will find and ask you will get. Will never be disheartened for not having money for start-up. Be a professional.

Now, choose what kind of business you want to do. Find any material according to your local's availability for your business. As we live in different places, different climates, the natural resources are different. Choose according to your place your business. OK, in the meantime, here I suggest your kinds of people. I call them average people.

Average people are the people:

1. People who want the hard work.
2. People who do not like to work.
3. People who fear to work and shy because of born in high social status family.
4. People who don't know what work they have to do.

I call them average people. Most of them work hard and they live in same conditions. People who want work, they love to work, they work hard but they revolve round the work. They earn money and they finish the money what they have earned hard.

Another group of people who don't like to work. They depend their existence of their life on their family and parents. They are easy going to work. They don't want to work. They don't like to take any risk in the long run. They need to be elevated and motivated. They are happy go luck. The third kind of people are the people who fear to work. Because they think they are well educated so they think low profile works are not suitable for them. And some high family group - they think my parents are high class and my class is high we don't want this low kind of work such as labour, company workers, and hard earning work Actually, they fear what other people will say and talk about them if they work such jobs.

Among them also their people who are afraid to work because they think that they can't do this work, they won't be able to do that work. They are shy people. And some are clan's hierarchy mentality.

The fourth group of people are the people who don't know how to do and what kind of work they will do. I was; also did not know what I should for my living, for my expenditure. I jump from one work to another. No fruit I got at all.

The above groups of people I call average people. This group of people consisted 80% of the total population of the world.

Some of them earn by joining in other company or small workshops, hotels, in small industry and by running small vendors such as vegetable vendors and some other earn by doing handicrafts works.

They earn money only for living. Their income is called earned income. They earn say Rs.8,000 to Rs.10,000 in some case it may be higher. They finish the earned income in maintaining such as electric bill, water bill, clothes, foods, and personal expenditure and tuition fee for his child. He earns monthly Rs.8,000 ($ 91.98) then Rs.8,000 is expended for the above expenditure. Now nothing is left. His balance is zero.

Sometime, by some reasons. Say illness be borrowed money from friends or relatives. Now he is in debt.

He is always in the treadmill life. Work and work. He/she works hard but can never come up from that cycle. He is always unhappy, anguish, in sad mood. This is not always in all cases.

And young people earn and spend their money. Spend the life in happy go lucky manner.

To escape from this hard-earned money lifestyle and never climb up from that level. We need to earn passive income.

In the passive income level, you can earn extra income by which means you can climb up and up.

The following is the diagram how the average people spend their money:

Diagram (1)

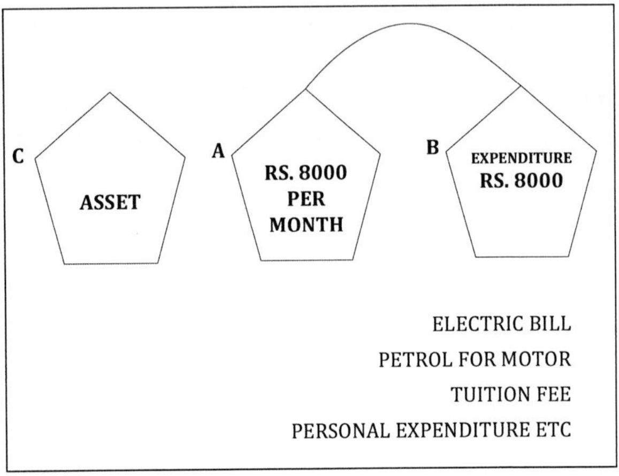

In the above diagram we know that a person earns Rs.8000 ($96.48) per month by working 7 hours a day. This is called earned income. The house A. and in the house B the person spent all his money in paying electric bill, petrol for his bike, tuition fee for his child and some for his personal expenditure, etc. To meet all these expenses his earned income is all expended. Non nothing is left. Sometimes due to illness he borrowed money from friends or relatives. Now he is in debt. He puts nothing in the house C (ASSET HOUSE). This house is income producing house.

In the above diagram the arrow indicates that the person earns hard by working 7 hours a day directly passes to the expenditure house.

It does not pass through the Asset house fig. C. Earns money and finish it al. Then he lives in treadmill lifestyle. Working hard but nothing is improved. He lives in this cycle of working hard and spend all.

Now Diagram (2)

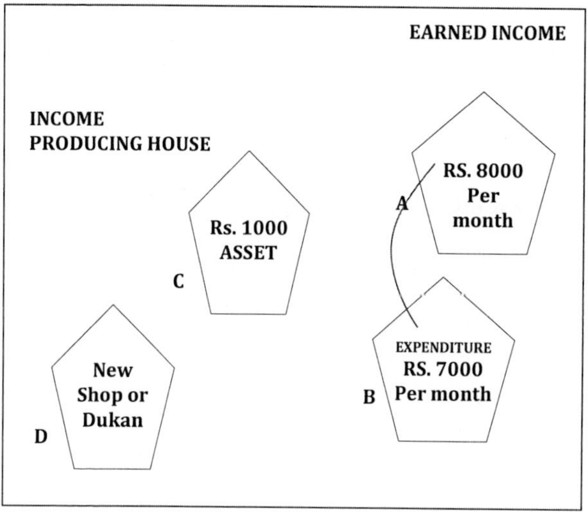

In the above diagram, we know that the person X saves Rs.1,000 and spends Rs.7,000 per month. Thus, he puts Rs.1,000 in saving house C. He is ready for investment. Sometimes after he saves more money. He starts investment. He earns passive income the house C. Saving and saving he builds another house D. More income is coming to him. He now enjoys the life.

This is the way every rich people do. You might have heard many companies expanded all over country and all over the world. This is how the rich people work.

Yes, you also can do that. Be persistent, have determination, courage, and confidence. 'In your work, be always honest. Honesty brings you people trust.

Now, you may say Rs.8,000 ($ 96.48) earning and Rs.8,000 expenditure is compulsory.

I will suggest you some possibilities for building Asset House (C):

1. You may increase your working hours from 7hrs to 8hrs or 9hrs, i.e. 1hr to 2hrs a day for some months or years. So that you will earn extra money for saving.

2. **Marup** - a kind of system for raising capital. Here we form a group of ten people or 20 people. Say in group we form. Every one of us contributes Rs.1,000 each/month. The total money we contribute is Rs.10,000 (ten thousand) we give the money to any one of us. It is done by serial or lottery. After I" month, the second turn we all contribute Rs.1,000 each. The total amount Rs.10,000 is given to 2'd person who won the lottery or the person on the serial. Here the first person who got first Rs.10,000 will contribute Rs.1,000 plus some minimum interest says Rs.50 (Rs.1,000 + Rs.50). Likewise, the 2" person will also do the same. It is done till the turn is complete. The person who organises the marup will take the first turn. After the turn is complete. A new marup can be started.

3. Another way is by making a list of friends and relatives and neighbours. Say, make a list of one hundred persons from your friends and relatives. Choose by tick from the list the person who are rich and willing to lend you the money. Say list of 40 friends and relatives from 100 persons you selected. Then ask them to lend the money. Don't ask to one person only. Ask a little money from them all, one by one till you raise your required money for investment.

Don't fear. Be positive. There are many people who want to help other. So come out from your homeostatic conditions. Build your own business.

So, there are many possibilities for capital formation. Seek you will find, knock the door will open, ask you will get. 80% of the world population are in the average group of people - who love working hard but living at the same level, people who fear to work, and people who don't know what to do.

We urgently need to form groups of people to lead and guide the average people to have passive income. And groups of people, I mean, who are already in the passive income level or experts in this field.

Some suggestions what can be taken up for earning side income besides his/her earned income.

I suggest here: Making garlic paste, ginger paste, local spices packing's, poultry, growing lemon, apple, making Achar (pickles) growing king chilly (**u-Morok**), **Ngari** (dry fish fermentation), besan making, candle making noodles making, soap making, small chula making, Dry goose berry making, etc. And see what are available in your local areas that can be started with small capital. At the start do it alone, later hire people, then expand gradually.

Now a day many new products are showing up. See it, make your own product.

It is called change. Know your market.

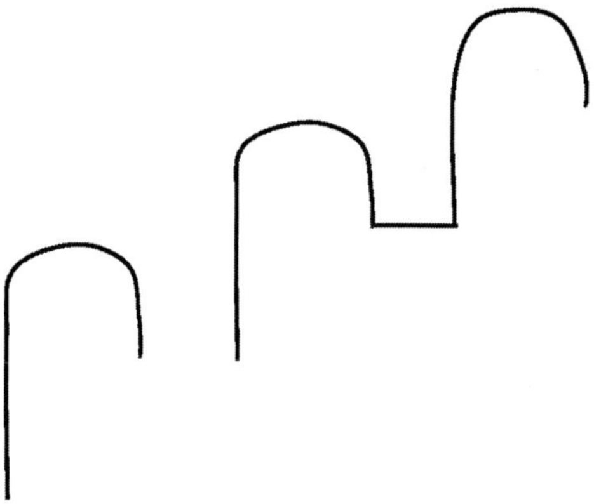

I say again, we are revolving round in the earned income way of life. Average people earn say, Rs. 8000/ month then he spends all they have earned. Now balance is zero. Nothing is left. He is always in poor conditions. We have to change this way of earning. Because we need extra income what we call passive income for our safety and security.

In the picture above, passive income way so step. This is the hardest part of building passive income in business.

Next when or after you establish passive income house your life is smooth and you are happy. In the above diagram the passive income way is smooth.

Next your business will face a turn or blind corner as shown above. In this area your business will face uncertain to period or trouble time. It is because of natural calamities or artificial disturbances. And your work is disturbed. It may also be due to high competition. In these times your savings may help you.

In this stage you should be clam, patient, perseverant, you should be resilient.

Failure or trouble time is compulsory. Nobody goes smooth in their business, you might have witness these many cases.

As you progress on your business you have passive income on rapidly increasing way. As you go on, suddenly you will face a decline in your business. During down time you need back up- or change your business where you need your savings you had and relationships you already established, you need to be resilient, courage, goal oriented.

Many shops are closed and new shops in that place come up. This is because of competition; new products replace old products.

We know that many company produces many new products replace old products.

We know that many companies produce many new products. We know that many companies produces many new products. These things also happen in small and medium scale industries.

Here that your savings and see I say the future are important to survive. Try to improve your product and try to produce new quality products. More exposure is required for new ideas.

OK, now start your own business anyway: any business suitable to you. There is nothing to be shame to do small start-up. Many people do it. They start small and build the Empire. Do come out from homeostatic state. Don't worry. First time experience is a bit uncomfortable and slow. Always remember extra mile, extra hours for your success.

Note: Many people in the passive income level failed in the management of life. One example is people who work in the govt. job earning passive income failed their life before or after retirement. After retirement they don't know how to manage their money.

In business we learn management of money. So businesspeople are happy.

Now, the following chapter I will write significant elements needed for doing business successful and its reward.

REMEMBER THAT BUSINESS IS NOT SIMPLY TRANSACTIONS OF THINGS – BUT IT IS A WAY OF LIFE – "MANAGING MONEY SUCCESSFULLY FOR HAPPY LIVES"

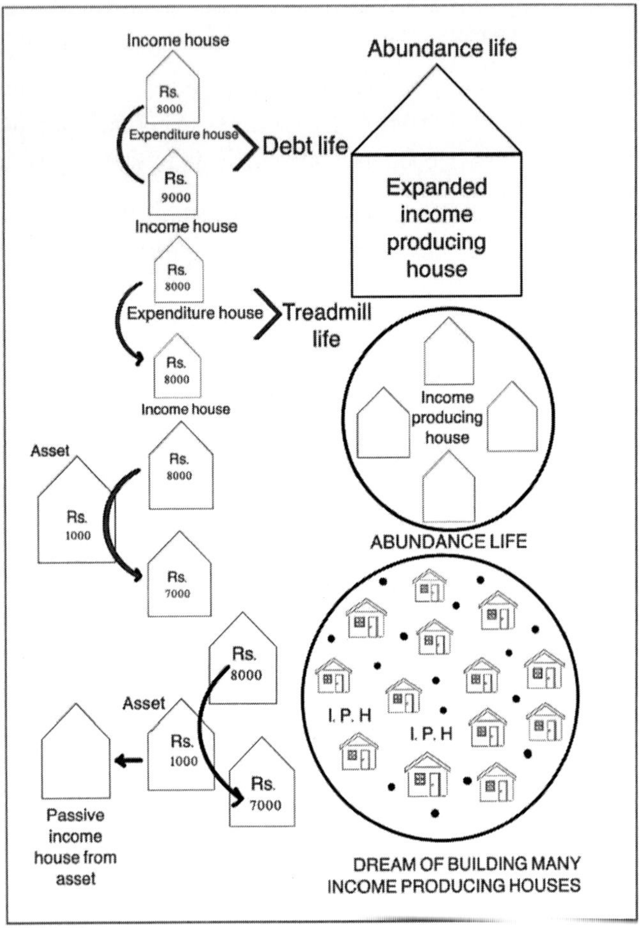
Income house
Rs. 8000
Expenditure house
Rs. 9000
Debt life
Abundance life
Expanded income producing house
Income house
Rs. 8000
Expenditure house
Treadmill life
Rs. 8000
Income producing house
Income house
Asset
Rs. 8000
Rs. 1000
Rs. 7000
ABUNDANCE LIFE
Rs. 8000
Asset
Rs. 1000
Rs. 7000
I. P. H
I. P. H
Passive income house from asset
DREAM OF BUILDING MANY INCOME PRODUCING HOUSES

CHAPTER – 8
RESPECT AND RECOGNITION

In the struggle of life's journey, you had many challenges. As you following the above principles as I discussed chapters.

As you flow on towards the stream of life's journey of happiness you gain knowledge and experiences, practices, hard struggle. Then you gain the fame and recognition of people and appreciation also for your contribution to the people and world.

Everybody like appreciation and recognition. He/she may work big or small. In spite of having huge amount of money he/she will not satisfy his life's journey. He/she may have good profession still he will lake recognition.

As you know everyone's inner's eagerness to have impact or fame.

It depends on your work, hard struggle incessant effort. Don't wait for fame. It will naturally come to you when you work honestly and persistently.

Have a goal, choose your professions – one or two, not more than three – pursue it. Be successful and get your fame and recognition.

CHAPTER – 9
HONESTY

The basic requirement in business success is honesty. Also in relationships honesty is a very essential element. The return of being honest is very great. If you are honest, people will believe you. So also customers will do the same. This means that honesty is a part in building your business success. Being honest your life will be in peace. But today, in modern age honesty, is a big issue. Most of us are not willing to be honest.

They like to possess things, money by dishonest means. Therefore, people like quick money. They get it. They live in hollow big building.

Any way tries to be honest if you want to be happy and live in peace. This peace, this happiness everyone covets to have in their lives.

However, do they forget it; why do they forget happiness! This is the problem.

Nothing is lost when you are honest. Be honest. Get peace.

When people get money by something dishonest means, on the next turn they will lose something of theirs in a big way. So be honest in your work, in your earning. You will get people's help. They will trust you, respect you. Honest people always make commitment. They fear to break his words or promises.

CHAPTER – 10
DREAM AND GOALS

What is your dream? Know and choose your life's dream. Dream means – Dreams are something (idea of liking profession - a big) which you want to achieve. That you create in your mind that can take any shape or from. Say for example, your idea of expansion of your business all over the world. This is a big dram.

And goals are based on taking action of your work what you want to achieve for your dream in your life. Have a big dream. Have a great hope. Dream is your lifelong journey. Be a big businessperson, a great producer of such as herbal medicine, or something else you want, like great as Amul Company, Tesla, Mc Donald.

Now, goal is in your hand, Example-you work on producing soaps, baskets, or both. Your goal is to sell your products to all over your local area, and then to your constituency. By and by you target to sell your products all over your state and country. Bigger the goal, bigger the dream is.

To attain your goal, you need a target. Target will be divided into hours, days, months, and years as to achieve your goal.

Without target you will be strayed way frequently from goal. So, make target your goal according to your convenience.

If you don't have a goal, you live a confused life. If you have no goal, you have no destination. Know your destination. General masses have no goal. So have a goal. Your goal is in a time frame.

Repeat yourself: ***"I HAVE A GOAL A BIG DREAN I GET MY DREAM THROUGH THE COMPLETION OF MY GOALS AT HANDS NOW."***

CHAPTER – 11
FEAR

Yes, fear is a natural quality that everybody possesses. There are different kinds of fears - a few I mention here are: fear of death, fear of starvation, fear of starvation, fear of losing job, fear of public speaking and fear of rejection.

Sure, I am afraid of public speaking in public. If tremble to speak before public. I forget what was in mind and forget what today.

So, do you do that? Right?

So, I shall write fear of 'rejection' and 'starvation'.

People fear and feel shame to ask what the need from other. Because they fear that they will be rejected. There is no need to dear of refection. If you are sky to be big, to ask, thing you what from others, you will thing you want from others, you will thing you want from others, you will fail your business. We live in a highly competitive world. Avoiding fear of rejection is a must. People who challenge rejection got success in most cases.

We need job security, working hard to earn more money. This is because of fear of starvation.

Ask, do works to get what you want. Never fear, learn more. Now time is changed, but we live in a new world with the old fashion change you concept. Do any work that produces income. Shop depending on family while you are strong, having the capability of earning.

To control fear, I guest, we need to leave some amount of eccentricity, that will good us to perform a work we want to do. Having a goal is also good to start our business.

Here eccentricity I mean in the sense that we can direct our attention to our goal without fearing what other will say and laugh at. Therefore, we know that fear is the negative element in starting up our business.

CHAPTER – 12
PATIENCE AND PERSEVERANCE

Failure or set back is compulsory one ought to face in the journey of life specifically in business. We will fail many times in our business efforts as Thomas Edison, Henry Ford etc. did. They were very patient to achieve their goals. They were to go ahead in-spite of failures.

So be patient and perseverant. At the start, your failure will be in your way, with business don't feel disappointed. Failure is a part of bringing success. You should be willing to be patient and perseverant to try again and again to achieve your goal, you larger goal.

At the start business is tough because we are novice. We have to learn many things and principles, techniques that are necessary in doing our business. Don't be quick in work at the starting. We need experiences.

At the start of your business, when you fail first time. Be patient and perseverant. Don't quit. "Quitter fails winner never quits".

I don't say to repeat what you fail first. I explained you to try another way that works for you to achieve your goal. Leave the failed part as experience and experiments.

Try to build your passive income house any way.

CHAPTER – 13
COURAGE & DETERMINATION

Courage and determination in the journey of life we will face many challenges. As you climb up for attaining happiness you may face rejection, discouraging situation. Down turn etc. In all these conditions you need to have courage. Courage is just opposite of fear. Fear makes you to slow your works, disturbs your progressive works, your efforts.

So, you need to have courage to challenge all those obstacles. Courage is inside you. You have to nurture it, bring up outside to face the challenges.

Without courage you cannot withhold the pressures, distractions from many angles from your environment as well as internal conflicts such as fear, anxiety, confusion, worry, negation. Courage is essential in attaining all elements of success and happiness I wrote above chapters.

To know more about courage, I refer to the book "The Courage" by Ruben Gonzales.

Avoid fear of rejection and face the fear of public speaking. One of the important things to develop Courage is that do the thing you fear the most. Fear will vanish. This is your courage.

Practice challenging in a good way to take out 'Courage' from within determination is very powerful energy to accomplish your task.

*Repeat yourself: "**I AM COURAGOUS, I AM COURAGOUS, I DO THING COURAGOUSLY, HONESTLY.**"*

CHAPTER – 14
TIME

Time is precious gift of nature. We come on earth truth time. We will pass away through timc. While leaving we have to do something good.

Past time is gone, it will never come back. . So, time is very precious and very important in our life. We exist on time. We because children, we were happy, we played and ate happily. We knew nothing about life.

We learn many things during that time. We were taught by parents and elders and teachers.

This is the proper time for children to be taught to have a dream. Slowly time go on we all become adult from teenage. In adult time we have the responsibility to work hard for our goals.

What will we do now? Yes, we have 24 hours a day gifted by nature.

Briefly, we use these ours say: 2 hours we use brushing teeth, bathing, exercise and breakfast. For working or reading we use 2 to 3 hours. Sleeping hours. For students- reading hours.

I specially discuss for workers and hard earners, so, then 8 hours for work time. Some time for rest. I shorten this time use because a lengthy explanation will give you boring. Then, sleep time is 7 to 8 hours. It varies from person to person according their convenience.

Sometime we also need to engage in other works, such as social works, social gatherings, sharing for friends and relatives ceremonies. We must use time cautiously and wisely. Loose time use means loses of your opportunities and less money earning. Loose time use also means that you don't have goal.

We are not aware of thinking time. Take care time. Don't wait your work for tomorrow.

If you work 8 hours a day you will get income of 8 hours. But in modern time (age) the concept of time compounding brings forth. Try to use time compounding concept.

See your future. Work for your years to come, work for your old age. Use time wisely and enjoy time. By positive way of thinking. Have some hours to work, make your time for working, dining, exercise, leisure, etc. Take proper time for sleep. Successful people do it.

But for attaining your goal use time properly not burn out yourself, so manage your time according to your condition. Time management is really necessary for attaining your goal and happiness.

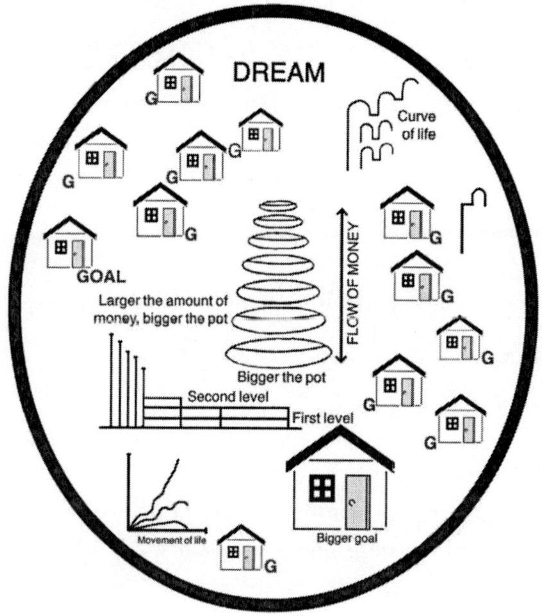

Note: Make your pot bigger. Bigger the pot (receptacle), i.e. your mind, will retain big money.

Smaller the pot (receptacle), you mind, will retain small amount of money- so make it a bigger pot for your richness.

To attain your goal accomplished make your target write it down:

i. Daily target,

ii. Weekly, monthly and so on. Daily target: waking up on time, your food time, house hold time, and work time to accomplish in a day. Including your leisure time also.

CHAPTER – 15
REPEAT BY YOURSELF

Nowadays it seems to lack of love and self-respect among us; serious crises, are happening in our human societies.

So, respect yourself and others. Love yourself and others too.

You will be rich and happy

REPEAT

To attain success and happiness and bring welfare for others also. Repeat and speak loudly or silently the following words by yourself:

1. I love myself and I love others.

2. I respect myself and I respect others.

Discrimination is one of our challenges; by love and respect can reduce impartiality.

I also repeat by heart: "I am happy and healthy and wealthy, young and beautiful".

Really it works for me. Why not for you too! Try it

Compose sentences in positive ways, according to your wants.

Yes, only positive words, negative words shouldn't be included.

3. If you want to be rich in terms of money. Repeat, "I love money, I receive money abundantly every day and money also loves me, thank you- MONEY." Repeat this frequently as you can.

ABOUT THE AUTHOR

Nighthoujam Basanta Singh (alias Thouren) is a multifaceted person with a passion for reading, paintings, and indoor games. Holding an MA in political Science, he draws inspiration from Blue Rose Publishers. Despite struggling with writing, he has authored two books, "Where you are!" and where you are! Part-II - Lit Up Your Lamp." Driven by a strong desire to contribute to society, he continues to write and share his knowledge and experiences, particularly on inspiration.

Although shy and hesitant to present himself in front of an audience, his inner voice encourages him to push beyond his comfort zone. Recognising the importance of effective communication, he is working to improve his public speaking skills, aiming to confidently share his ideas and connect with his audience. With persistence and dedication, he strives to make a meaningful impact through his writing and sharing of inspiration. His journey reflects a commitment to personal growth and a little contribution to the community.

ABOUT THE BOOK

As we continue the live as a social being we now need to improve our living conditions. For this purpose, I would like to contribute my share at utmost to the society. I would like to keep peace and harmony among ourselves without distinction of creed or castes.

To achieve this, I write the second volume of the book,

'Where you are! Part-II

- Lit up your lamp.'

Where you are! I would like to mean that one's social condition among our human society. There are seven main elements which a person must possess for his/her success and happiness.

Possessing of seven elements one is to be considered successful and happy.

And Lock of any one or two or more in his/her personality is "Where you are!"

Fulfilment of all seven elements on one's life means **"Where you are!"**

For this sake I suggest you my respected readers to start your business. Business not now a days a mere production and selling of products. It becomes a way of life one should learn it because it is a way of life without which it will mean a failure of life. Successful business really becomes skill in life's management.

Management of life will mean a success in one's life and happy forever.

If you do not teach what you learnt to your relatives, you will lose your legacy. Teach what you know to your people.